I

MATTER

THE VOICES OF

SURVIVORS

Table of Contents

FOREWORD

This book is filled with strong and powerful women. Each brave enough to share their stories and hope it will be a light in the darkness. Each chapter is raw and beautiful. The women in this book chose to be vulnerable and open. To let you see into their pain and their stories.

If you are being abused please reach out to local agencies and get help. No one male or female deserves to be abused and no one is to blame for others behavior.

OUR PRAYER FOR YOU
Clara Peters

The LORD has done it this very day; let us rejoice today and be glad. As stated in **Psalm 118:24 Amen**

Father God I come to you as a humble servant saying thank you. Thank you, Father, for being you for always being in our lives... You give us all we need daily to continue to press our way in life.

Father as I come in prayer I come asking for strength, healing, peace, joy, and happiness continuously for those that is walking out their life from being abused by a Love one.

I am praying for your daughters as they in need as they say I am all that my father says I am. Father your word says in **Psalm 139:14 "I praise you, for I am fearfully and wonderfully made. [a] Wonderful are your works; my soul knows it very well".**

Father you are omnipotent one to help in stopping the hurt that women may feel Father help her to see that she is a

Proverbs 31:10 as it states [a] An excellent wife who can find? She is far more precious than jewels. Help her to understand the husband that is ordained for her will never hurt her. Father, thank you for showing her that she is worthy to be a wife that she is a woman of worth and that you will continue to give her all she needs to be all you have ordained her to be in this life.

Father help her to walk with her head held high as she has nothing to be ashamed of help her to know that, *Psalm 30:5 says "For his anger is but for a moment, and his favor is for a lifetime. [A] Weeping may tarry for the night, but joy comes with the morning"* and when that joy comes understand it will be that she seeks.

I thank you Lord for helping those that are needing healing even more so Father as they are weak give them strength they need to get up as they have not finished the purpose driven life you have for them.

Father give her that peace, as stated in *Philippians 4:7 says, "And the peace of God, which surpasses all understanding, will guard your hearts and your minds in Christ Jesus." Amen.* Show her father that you are her peace to always seek you.

Father help her to know that each morning she awakens there's an assignment she must walk out. Help her to see that you will restore her Father, as you wrap your arms around her at night and whisper in her ear *"And we know that all things work together for good to them that love God, to them who are the called according to his purpose as stated in* **Romans 8:28. Amen**

Father I end this prayer thanking you for granting us the freedom to walk in peace and not pieces. I thank you for showing us the truth and the light as we walk in healing from abuse. Father we love you as you didn't have to give us another chance but you love us just that much. Father I decree and declare that each woman that reads this that each woman that is in need of your help believe that it is done right now in the name of Jesus. Father I decree and declare that all her dreams and desires are going forth according to your will as you have released her from bondage. Father I thank you as we lay our burdens at the altar for you and to never pick back up.

Father help her to know that she should always do what thus said the word according to **Matthew 6:33 "But seek ye first the kingdom of God, and his righteousness; and all these things shall be added unto you."** *as you will never stir her wrong.*

Allow her to understand that no matter what as it is stated in **Matthew 7:7 "Ask and it shall be given you; seek, and ye shall find; knock and it shall be opened unto you***:" as your will not; Come back to us void. I thank I praise and I honor for it all as you have set us all free to be that woman you have created us to be.*

*In Jesus name I decree and declare **VICTORY** in these beautiful daughters as they continue to walk in peace joy happiness and love. **Amen***

Women of Divine Distinction **(W.O.D.D.)** is about **EMPOWERING** and **ENCOURAGING** women to be all that they can be and let them know that they have a voice. Letting each woman know that failure is not an option, so go out and receive that purpose that **GOD** has just for you. To help redefine, renew, and restore what has been lost.

Woman of God it is your time to spread your wings and soar.....use that voice and be the mighty woman that you were born to be.

2 Corinthians 3:12-18 Therefore, since we have such a hope, we are very bold. We are not like Moses, who would put a veil over his face to prevent the Israelites from seeing the end of what was passing away. But their minds were made dull, for to this day the same veil remains when the old covenant is read. It has not been removed, because only in Christ is it taken away. Even to this day when Moses is read, a veil covers their hearts. But whenever anyone turns to the Lord, the veil is taken away. Now the Lord is the Spirit, and where the Spirit of the Lord is, there is freedom. And we all, who with unveiled faces contemplate[a] the Lord's glory, are being transformed into his image with ever-increasing glory, which comes from the Lord, who is the Spirit. WOMAN OF GOD, go after your Freedom as stated in verse 17 and be that mighty WOG you were designed to be. Stop sitting quietly as your life passes you by, get up and claim what GOD has just for you. AMEN

About the Author

Clara Peters is a Pastor, mother of 3, grandmother of 7, radio talk show host, motivational speaker, mentor, certified life coach, certified peer recovery coach, International Bestselling Author, Board Certified Christian Counselor, and Blogger. She is a woman of Integrity; **Founder of 'Clara L Peters Ministries/Founder of 'Women of Divine Distinction Ministry.'** You can find her on **Facebook** under her name **Clara L Peters** and her fan page, **Author Clara L. Peters. Founder of Divine Diva Book Club**, if you would like to be a part of the book club, You can send her a PM on Facebook. For Speaking Engagements you can contact her Via Facebook or email her at: atclarapetersministries@yahoo.com or call 1-832-490-9211.

MY SHATTERING
Teresa Hawley Howard

My story starts the same as many others! I fell in love with an older man. I was sixteen and he was twenty-five. I was young and naïve and did not know what love was. Or what relationships were supposed to look like or feel like. I just knew that love was enough to change him and for us to live happily ever after.

Nothing could have been further from the truth. I went into this relationship with an open and loving heart. It was my first relationship and my first love. But I was not equipped for what was coming. I had no idea what I had gotten myself into.

It started with emotional and verbal abuse. He would call me names, tell me how stupid I was, tell me I was never going to be anything in life. I was so isolated by the time the first physical incident happened that I did not know how to react. I was sitting in our truck with him and telling him how I wanted to buy a baby bed for our first born. I was about 6 months pregnant at the time. He had to told me several times to shut up and be quiet. But I did not stop. I stated I make money and I want to use it buy things for the baby. This just made him madder. Yes, I made money but he kept it all. And he reached across and slapped me into the door of the truck. I was so shocked. And I was so surprised that I did not know how to react.

I should have left then, but I did not. I had another child with him and the abuse escalated and continued. There were so many that I can not count them. But I hid them and lied about them. I covered for him. He went to jail, I bailed him out. I was sure if I was just a better wife, a better mom, a better person, then he would stop. But it did not. It was only getting worse.

By the time I finally left both my girls were grown, and I had two grandkids. In hindsight, I wish I had stayed gone the first time I left him. But we all know that hindsight is 20/20. And we can not change the past. We can only learn from it and move on. I hope by sharing some of my story that someone else will get out and get help!

When I left, I had to pick up the shattered pieced of my life, my pride, and me. I had to learn to rebuild my life. I had to find myself and who I was now. The little girl he married was gone and now I needed to find out who the woman in her place was now.

About the Author

Teresa Hawley-Howard is an international best-selling author and publisher. Her mission in life is to help others find their voices and share their stories! She also wants to help them walk through their pain, limitations, and their own doubt to live the life they deserve. She knows their words, stories, scars, and their pain can inspire, heal and give hope to another person.

She is an empowerment/writing coach, publisher, speaker, #1 international best-selling author, radio host, and CASA volunteer.

She is also Co-Founder of Tribute Magazine, Founder of Global Inspirations Magazine and New & Noteworthy Magazine, Radio Host of The Mission Radio show, and host of Modern-Day Woman and Words Have Power Podcasts! She is also a blogger at Thrive Global. Founder of WOM Enterprises Publishing and Promotion, helping others to find their voice and share it with the world.

WOM Enterprises offers complete publishing packages for authors! The company offers several ways to become an author! You can write in one of many anthologies or you can write your own book! Either way you will become a published author! Share your story, promote your business and create your legacy! WOM Enterprises will help you make your dream become a reality. So, stop procrastinating and become an author today with WOM Enterprises!

Reach out and let Teresa help you share your story!

www.teresahawleyhoward.com
teresa@takeactionwithteresa.com
fb Teresa Hawley Howard
Twitter @teresahawleyhoward
Instagram @writinghealsyoursoul

NOT ALL SCARS ARE PHYSICAL
Amy L Fordyce

I struggle with writing this story as I did for another Anthology. One, because I'm really a private person just close family and friends know. Two, I only gave a brief glimpse into the abuse I suffered. I know a few people didn't want me to write that story and I'm sure this glimpse will also not go over well in this book, but it is my story to share. I stopped letting people run my life when I got out of this relationship. I am my own person and not someone's property. I've had several relationships that had some type of abuse in them. Whether it was Emotional, Verbal, Physical, Financial or Sexual abuse, but one had it all. If I write the full view of this one relationship it would take up a whole book. Like all relationships do, this one started out fine. No red flags. Showing what you would expect as good side of someone. Only what a full blown Narcissist would do. This person is the poster individual of Narcissistic Personality Disorder.

1. Has a grandiose sense of self-importance.
2. Is preoccupied with fantasies of unlimited success, power, brilliance, beauty, or ideal love.

3. Believes he or she is special and unique and can only be understood by or should associate with other special or higher status people.
4. Requires excessive admiration.
5. Has a sense of entitlement.
6. Is interpersonally exploitative and takes advantage of others to achieve his or her own means to ends.
7. Lacks empathy is unwilling to recognize the feelings or needs of others.
8. Is often envious of others or believes that others should be envious of them.
9. Shows arrogant, haughty behaviors or attitudes.

I didn't take notice when he started separating me from family members. He had gone as far as to send nasty messages to my Mom using my phone like they were from me. Thank goodness she had figured that one out. It did take her a little time though to realize it.

In just a few short months into the relationship all that changed. He started accusations that I was cheating in the relationship with of all people a cousin of mine. That night just before I left for work he choked me until I stopped breathing. I came to and couldn't actually believe what happened. I gathered my things and just left work. I had marks around my neck. Just covered them up best I could with makeup. All the while him texting me saying how sorry he was never happen again. Stupid me believed him. This started the year of more abuse and all kinds of accusations.

Started with the name calling after the night he choked me. I have been called everything under the sun or anything you could image when my grandmother passed way. The evening of her visitation he kept texting me when I would be home and I wasn't at the funeral home I was out cheating; same thing during the funeral. All in between these events I also continued to work my night shifts. No sleep was to be had.

It got to the point I was forced to go to work day shift. I preferred nights because I'm basically a night owl anyways always have been. I don't sleep at night now cause of the pain I'm in from the Injuries I had sustained from the abuse hard to get comfortable.

I never had a good day at work. As soon as I would leave the driveway the nasty messages would begin. Anything from him having a bad dream I was in that I did something so it must be true. If you didn't answer him fast enough you were basically in for it. He even came out to my job site a few times because of it. Which according to him I didn't have a job. Even with having a pay stub to prove it and he was at my job sites before. It just became much easier to just agree with everything that he said. The beatings were not as bad as when you tried defending yourself. Still bad enough though. This individual even became extremely jealous of my deceased husband. To the point of not understanding why there was an age difference between us. He even started to abuse his memory. I removed from my home all memories I had of my late husband and put them in the safe hands of my Mom.

One weekend in the fall of this relationship everything went to way too far. I should also mention this person had a major alcohol problem along with abusing prescription medications. I ended up going to the Emergency Room that weekend.

I'm not even sure what had started the weekend going wrong. But I ended being thrown downstairs up against appliances, counter tops, also my truck. I was choked numerous times which was his favorite thing to do to me.
I grabbed a few things when I could get away from him and left. I went and hide at friend's house. I knew if I went anywhere that he knew from family leaves it wouldn't have been the end of the beating. The next day I went to my Moms. She went to the hospital with me I had X-rays done just to check for broken bones. The hospital called the Police and they filled charges.

To say that was the end of the relationship it wasn't. The charges were dropped. He had to move back to the state of West Virginia because he was on parole. To this day I've never completely learned the truth behind that. But I'm sure he didn't tell me the truth.

Once again I have to say I fell for the "it'll never happen again crap." He convinced me to move to West Virginia in with a friend of ours and transfer job sites. The abuse didn't stop there till one night he went too far with stuff and our friend called the Police had him taken in. She took me in and had a Protection from Abuse Order put against him. I'm grateful for doing that. Till this day though; I'm still convinced that this individual may not be done with me. Time will only tell.

The damage that I have from this abuse is three herniated discs in my back. The damage to my throat, making swallowing difficult at times leading to choking which is scary when home alone. I have a partial plate for my lower front teeth that was cracked I've had side teeth removed because they were pushed in. I have hearing aids for my left ear because of the inner damage to it. Abuse of any kind is not Ok. It causes lasting affects; 'Physically and Emotionally' Un-learning abuse also means unlearning the abuse behaviors that you inherited as survival tactics. If you have to, get help where you can.

About the Author

Amy grew up on small family farm in Greene County, Southwestern Pennsylvania. Her family raised everything from rabbits to cattle and horses. She was raised with the value of 4-H standards where she held leadership positions. She has a strong passion for animals. Amy has showed horses since childhood where she won many awards and taught youth proper horse care and riding. She has raised, bred, and shown her own American Quarter Horses and American Paint Horses, along with cattle; with her family and her late husband. She has worked for the Washington County Human Society; Also for a local Greene County Animal Hospital. For many years she has worked for top Security Companies in Pennsylvania for the Oil and Gas Fields; also local coal mines. It was in this industry, where she met her current husband and second soul-mate. Yes true love can find you twice. Amy currently lives in the beautiful country side of Southwest Pennsylvania/Northern

Panhandle of West Virginia, with her husband Larry and family pets cat Lanko :found as a tiny kitten on a gas well site who thinks he`s a dog. Three lovable sweet dogs: Rascal the tiny Chihuahua; Squeaker the princess Dachshund, and Cami: the diva mixed bred, and her American Quarter Horse she raised Zippos Front Page aka "Duke". Amy works as best she can with a nonprofit horse rescue Save a Horse Stable in Sycamore Pa, when her health permits.

Amy`s first story about the horse rescue '*Angel`s Among Shattered Souls"* in her first Anthology '*Angels Among Us Devotional*' '*Whisper`s of Love, Light, and Blessings*' went to Best Seller. Amy also has a second story out in the Anthology '*From Broken to Beautiful - Owning Your Truth,*' And is currently available on Amazon.

Contact Info:
Email: amyswanigereaton@yahoo.com
P.O. Box 163 Graysville, PA. 15337

10 THINGS I WISH I KNEW ABOUT ABUSE
Chou Hallegra

We often only talk about physical abuse because it's easy to identify, when see it. Where we see bruises, blood, and cuts, it's easy to say: "This person is being abused." However, there are many people, male and female, suffering in silence because they don't recognize that what they are going through is indeed abuse. I was in an emotionally abusive relationship for years and didn't even realize it and it greatly affected my mental health in a negative way. If a person is subjecting or exposing another person to behavior that may result in psychological trauma, including anxiety, chronic depression, or post-traumatic stress disorder, then we have a case of emotional abuse, sometimes referred to as psychological abuse.

Words do hurt and hurtful words can leave deep emotional wounds that affect how a person sees him or herself, and even how this person sees the world in general. I can't go go back into the past and change anything, but I can make sure my future, and yours is not impacted by this. I hope these ten things I've learned through my journey will either save you or protect you from abuse of any kind. My hope is that you will share this information with people you care about so that they are informed as well because knowledge is power.

1. Abuse is not always what we do. It can also be what we don't do.

For example, when Children & Youth Services do an investigation for neglect, why do they call it abuse? It's because something that was supposed to be done was not done. Sometimes people give each other the 'silent treatment.' How does that affect the other person? This happened to me more times than I can recall. If my partner wasn't happy about something, he would retreat in his own corner; totally act as if I was not in the house. Sometimes this went on for days. I started feeling that I didn't matter and that I was not worth his time.

2. True love is not earned

When people are affected by emotional or psychological abuse, they often get into the habit of trying everything they can to earn the person's love. Sometimes, there is nothing they can do that would actually make a difference. I remember trying to say the right thing, wear the right clothes, cook the right food, clean the right way, and the list went on and on. Unfortunately, everything I did was never good enough. My partner was still not happy and would continue to make me feel like I would never be enough. I wish I knew that I wasn't responsible for someone's happiness. I wish I knew that if someone loved me, I wouldn't have to work so hard at making them love or like me. People who love you would love you just the way you are. You don't have to earn their love nor their approval.

3. Emotional wounds often leave deeper scars than physical wounds.

I had times in the past that I thought to myself, "if only I had a bruise, a cut, or a broken limb, the injury would have healed by now." My injury was not healing as quickly as I wanted it to. It took years of pain and years of internal work, including counseling, to get me to where I am today. And there are still days I feel the sore spot in my heart that was left by the emotional wounds I have endured. They never heal all the way through. They are always tender, and have to be handled with care. These emotional wounds have traumatized me more than any physical wound I ever had. Having my tongue sewn back together doesn't even come close to the pain of emotional abuse.

4. Love is an active verb, not a passive one.

I remember hearing, "I love you," when everything was going his way, when he had what he wanted. Often it was his way or the highway. If he wasn't happy, someone was to blame and everyone must suffer as a result. That was his highway. It took me a long time to realize that's not love. When someone says he or she loves you but their actions says otherwise, do yourself a favor and listen to their actions and not their words. Action speaks louder than words. If they love you then their actions should prove it.

5. No human being can save another.

I used to tell myself, "Maybe if I prayed hard enough, he would change. Maybe if I was a better spouse, he would be one too." I tried to get him and us counseling, he wasn't interested. He didn't think we needed it. His response was, "If you do what you need to do as a wife, then we wouldn't have any problem." I thought I could save him. I worked in social services, I knew how to help people make better choices and help them get the help they needed, and surely I could do it in my own home!" or so I thought; and I was wrong. Even if he had gone to counseling, neither the counselor nor I could change him. People change when they realize that the pain of remaining the same is worse than the pain of changing. It's then and only then do they choose to change. They choose to change. They have to want to change, and then choose to change, in order to actually change. Nobody can do that for them but themselves.

6. Sometimes staying for the kids might cause more damage than you realize.

I didn't want my kids to grow up in a 'broken home,' so I stayed as long as I could. What I didn't realize is that the longer I stayed, the longer they were being impacted as well. Today, my oldest remembers things that I don't. She's seen and hurt more than she should at her age. All this resulted in an anxiety disorder. My younger children have a hard time trusting people, especially my middle child. They had witnessed the emotional abuse that I experienced and it created some emotional wounds in them as well. If only I had known! Today, five years later, they are happy kids and they are thriving. It made change in my narrative. My kids are not from a 'broken home.' They are not broken people. They are being raised in a loving home with consistency and security. If you're in an abusive home, know that your kids are being affected by that environment.

7. **Promises that are not kept today**
Become commitments that are not kept tomorrow. He would promise to do something with me and the kids and then find himself back on his computer. He would promise to do something for me, of something I wanted and then it would never happen. It was almost as if he slapped me in the face and said he wouldn't do it again, but then he does it again at the first opportunity he got. If you are dating someone and him or she is always showing up late, or not keeping up with things he or she committed to, that's a red flag to watch for.

If someone doesn't give you the time of day, don't think that things will miraculously change once they commit to you. What you see is often what you get, especially when it comes to 'not-so good' behaviors. If he or she cannot make time for you now, most likely that would be the case later as well. People do change, but do not commit to someone in the hopes that they would change. Make sure that you are comfortable with whom they are today and that you can live with that person as they are. Then, if they change, that's an added bonus. If they don't, at least you know what you are getting yourself into.
I saw many red flags before and didn't take them seriously. I thought things would change once we are in the same house. Things did change, not for the better but for the worse. The red flags became flashing red lights and I kept

telling myself, things will get better, things will get better. I wish I had taken the time to see if things would get better before I made a long-term commitment.

8. Both the abuser and the victim can be ignorant of the abuse.

I was ignorant to the abuse I suffered. The red flags were there. The flashing red lights were there. I thought, "We are just going through a hard time." Even when things became unbearable to the point I wish I was dead rather than keeping living this nightmare, I still didn't call it abuse. The accusations became insults. The silent treatment became abandonment. Even during a medical crisis, my ex acted as if I was not visible at all, and I was pregnant with our youngest child at the time. He barely saw the kids, although we lived in the same house. I would purposely leave the house when I got home from work and the kids got home from school. He worked night child but would leave many hours prior to his shift. It was as he was intentionally avoiding us. All this went on for months and months, and I still didn't call it abuse. It wasn't until months after I was out of the situation that I realized how emotionally damaged I was from this relationship. I couldn't value myself or appreciate my accomplishments. I would never speak up and let everyone walk all over me. It wasn't until much later that I realized that it all came from how I was treated in my marriage. I was told things like, "What are you going to say?" "You have nothing good to say anyway…" "People like you would go to hell because you are not a good wife…" "It's always your fault." Later on, I was even told, "You're a witch…" "You make me sick and I want to vomit." How can anyone have any appreciation for themselves after hearing things like this? After we were separated, I had very low self-esteem and never said a word even when I should, and I still didn't call it abuse. I work in human services and I should have known, right? Well, when you're in, it's hard to see it. You need to educate yourself and let healthy people speak truth to you. Of course my ex wouldn't call any of this abuse either; he still doesn't think he did all of these bad things to me. If you are not sure if what you're going through is abuse, this link will provide some insight and resources for you to get help:_ https://www.thehotline.org/is-this-abuse/abuse-defined/

9. Tomorrow might be too late.

We have all heard stories of people who died in the hands of their abuser. These stories are on TV, in the newspapers, on social media, etc… If you feel unsafe, please save your life and those of your children before things get worse. Constant rage can easily turn into physical abuse. Just because he or she is not leaving any marks on your body doesn't mean that you should stay. If you do not feel safe for any reason, please get out. Call 911. Don't worry about what you would leave behind; nothing is more important than life. After you leave, if the person gets help and truly changes, then it's up to you to decide if you want to give them a second chance, but please do get good counsel. Abuse is devastating, even when its abuse that nobody sees and you don't deserve to be treated that way.

10. **You are worth more than your experiences.** No matter what you've been through, no matter what you had to deal

with, no matter what your experiences have been; I want you to know that you are worth more than all of that. You are worth more than what happened to you. You can become more than the sum of your experiences. You can start a new life, you can still move forward with your life. Don't let your past steal your joy. Don't let your past steal your dreams. Don't let your past steal your life or your identity. Use your experiences to help others. I became a Counselor and then a Certified Trauma Professional after the abuse I endured. I don't want any child or teen to go through what I went through in my young years and I don't want any woman to be treated the way I was treated in my marriage. There is a way out. Help is available. There are resources to help you. Last but not least, don't let shame stop you from getting the help you need. A better life awaits, it's time to be free!

About the Author

Chou Hallegra is a Best-Selling Author, a Transformational Speaker, and a Certified Counselor, and Life Coach. She is committed to helping people achieve mental and emotional wellness, reach their full potential, and live fulfilling lives. Find out more at www.graeandhopeconsulting.com

FIGHT WITHIN THE RANKS
Rhonda Cee

What I am about to tell you is a story about one of the touchiest subjects that has ever transpired in the largest most secure organization in the Country. As old and taboo as this story is, it still has countless victims unable to overcome the fear of speaking out against such a violation and injustice. Despite the years of mental health counseling I continue to receive on a regular basis, I am still uncomfortable talking about it with strangers. Even though the first event happened several years earlier, it took me decades to feel confident that my story would one day be believed, let alone validated.

There were so many more incidences that took place after the first violation that I will have to piece it all together like a quilt of scraps. I did not fully understand what stress could do to a person's mental health since it was such a huge stigma that the thought of it was taboo. As a young private in the military, fresh out of high school, all I knew was that I could always trust my fellow soldiers to have my back, no matter the age, gender or rank. At least that is what I thought I was told. I admit I was a bit gullible and naïve as most young girls would be there first time away from home. I was probably more sheltered than I realized too. I learned about being an adult woman in a world full of men with hidden agendas. My eyes opened fast and my trust diminished just as quickly.

As a reservist, I went on two-week training missions with my hometown unit every year. My family was so proud of me because I was the oldest of my cousins, the first to go to college and join the military. I wanted to set a good example and be a success. One year, my squad of less than ten with only two of us being female, were divided up and assigned to an all-male combat field artillery unit. I thought it would be interesting to provide support to an Infantry unit. Not many females I knew could say that. They even allowed me and my two male squad members to fire one of the weapons too. I had no fear of being out there with all those men, because I trusted them to have my back. I never had any idea they would cause me harm, especially my own squad members who I worked with one weekend each month and two weeks out of the year. They knew me and I thought I knew them.

It had been a rough couple of days getting to our field point to set up our tents and supplies. We traveled in a convoy through the night for what seemed like days on the bumpiest road they could find. My squad members shared jokes and laughs in the back of the vehicle while trying to keep from falling on the floor. We were allowed to sleep, but that was impossible and dangerous due to the abrupt stops. Once you are propelled from a cot to the hard vehicle floor, you stay awake! We all had our rucksacks packed to the fullest and talked about the most important thing we wanted to do once we finished setting up our tents, TAKING A SHOWER! Since we were the support unit, we were given the opportunity to utilize the showers in a building close by, but it was a little further from the field site than expected. That was fine with us! A real shower was a treat and we were determined to find it and we did.

When we arrived, we found that there was only one building with showers. We thought there were two, one for males and the other for females. Since I was the only female, we agreed that they would go first while I stood outside until they were done. When they came out, they told me there was no shower curtain nor was there a way of securing the door to the building. I was new at this, so I did not think to check for any of these things and I trusted they knew what they were doing since they were more experienced. To keep me safe as my "battle buddies" the two males I had been on other field training exercises with in the past, but in actual hospitals or clinics offered to stand outside the building while I took my turn taking a shower just as they did before me.

As I started to get undressed, I had a feeling something was wrong, so I slowly turned around and to my surprise I saw one of them staring at me. I yelled out, "Ok, very funny. Now, stop!" I did not think for a minute that it was funny, but I was hoping he was only being an annoying butthead just giving me a hard time. He was the younger of the two and usually played around a lot more, which at times was a headache during our weekend drills. When he stepped back,

I hesitated for a minute to make sure he did not try that stunt again. After I felt comfortable to try undressing for the second time, I had a strange feeling that he was watching me again. This time they both were and had creepy smiles on their faces. I yelled, "STOP!", but they kept on. I yelled again, "TURN AROUND AND STOP LOOKING AT ME!" They kept staring and started laughing. That was the moment I first remember feeling alone and afraid. I was out there in the darkness with two males that I felt I could trust only minutes ago. All sorts of frightening things ran through my mind. I know I was a soldier, but I did not think I could win a fight against two males. There was nowhere for me to run and no one for me to call out to for help. I had to think of something, so I took a chance that they would not hurt me and turned my back to them so they would not see me look nervous. I remembered characters from the old westerns who said, "Never let them see you sweat." I was not sweating, but I was scared, and I did not want them to see that.

I had to stay strong and play the game as if what they were doing did not faze me. I hoped they would stop if I showed them that I was not afraid. I heard one of them tell me to go ahead and shower and they would stop watching or something like that. I was shaking in my boots. They still stood and watched me while I tried to figure out a way to shower without taking my BDU's off. Time was ticking and I decided to shower the best I could with my clothes on. My face and neck were the easy parts to wash. My shirt became drenched even more as I put the washcloth under it to clean my armpits. It was a good thing that the weather was warm, and I had a packed a couple of extra towels. Had this happened years later, I would have carried a pack of wet wipes with me at all times. Maybe this was the catalyst for me carrying a little of everything like MacGyver. The most challenging part of that shower was when I contemplated how I was going to maneuver the washcloth between my legs without unbuttoning my pants. Even though I recited the Twenty-third Psalm just like my grandmother taught me to do when I was afraid of the boogeyman or bullies at school, I still was not comfortable washing my private area not knowing if they were still watching me.

By the time I was done, they had stopped watching and were standing in the same area next to the building where I stood while they showered. A part of me had hoped they left me out there so I would not have to see them. They apologized and told me they were only joking. If a conversation was not about our jobs, I refused to make small talk with them or anyone else during the next few days. Being around a lot of those same males at that time, felt so uncomfortable for me; I did not have that issue before the shower incident. Several of them asked my squad members, who violated my trust, if I was on my period since my attitude had made such a big shift. That made me really mad and I could not tell them what happened. I was embarrassed and hurt and had to walk around with a not-so-fresh feeling. That would make anyone who enjoyed an opportunity for good hygiene awfully mad!

As soon as we returned to the rear, I spoke up to my entire squad. They had my back, remember? We were supposed to be family. Those two buttheads were the only ones who went against those principles. The look on everyone's face told me that they were going to be harshly punished, because this was clearly as case of harassment. We learned that in our company briefing before we left for the field exercise. I know what I heard! We all heard the same thing! Our Platoon Sergeant yelled at them, "Did you do that?" They admitted they did in front of our small squad. What surprised me was when the Platoon Sergeant told them not to do it again or they would be in big trouble. That was it. Immediately after, the squad to include the only other female started making jokes about it and saying that males do things like that and I could not take it seriously. Sometimes, I felt like it was too hard to hold back my tears, but I knew I had to. I also knew from that day forward; this was all a part of a bigger game and I had to learn to play it to survive. I just did not know how detrimental it was all going to be in the end.

Unfortunately, there were many more incidents of sexual harassment and other forms of abuse that happened to me and around me for years while I was in the military. Some of which I grew so desensitized to that I normalized it to some degree. Having no one believe that it happened to me was one thing, but what was even worse, in my opinion was the people who believed, but chose to ignore it. Way too often, I was expected to ignore it too and told to get over it. To this day, I feel like it will never end. I know that seems farfetched, but I lost hope a long time ago. Although I am not currently in a crisis, my mind and body stay in that mode. I have learned better coping techniques in order to be able to function in society to remain independent. I have been an emotional burden to my family and friends so much that I think it is safer for me to stay to myself more in order to minimize the risk of a trigger. This story of sexual harassment that I personally experienced was the first one to have happened to me, but it was far from the last. My mind plays tricks with me still to this day when it tries to convince me that I brought this type of abuse on myself each time it happened. I know the bad behavior of those males was never my fault, but it has taken me years of therapy to know when to tell my mind to shut the hell up, even though it does not always listen.

About the Author

As a 13-year veteran of the Armed Forces, I worked along my fellow soldiers as a Combat Medic and Avionics Repair Technician providing support to various units in the rear and during deployments. I experienced two decades in many career development areas such as a Human Resource Recruiter responsible for hiring the best possible employees that serviced a major fortune 500 company, a career counselor focused on preparing welfare-to-work recipients to sustain and maintain in self-sufficiency, a faith-based employment training entrepreneur collaborating with non-profit crisis organizations to assist in curbing the recidivism rate of criminal offenders and the disadvantaged population of young adults, and a housing manager for homeless veterans battling the similar issues of domestic violence, mental illness and substance abuse. My belief is that no matter how old you are, it's never too late to pursue your purpose. Throughout those various career endeavors, I battled with depression caused by verbal, mental and sexual assaults. While serious and sometimes crippling bouts of depression, I always kept that one little mustard seed of faith that I would conquer the demons of mental illness one by one to continue on my life's mission; to live free and bring a few others along for the victory party.

In the depths of my despair, my innermost belief is that changing the outlook, changes the outcome. I share not for the personal attention and definitely not for the pity, but for those injured souls who are just like me. You may say you can't do it, but I say with love, support and understanding and with someone who has been there, I say YOU CAN!

WHO AM I?
Sharon Gulley

My story is one of encouragement for those who like me were out in the world alone as a teenager and having to learn self love and appreciation, and survival. I questioned everything and everyone because of the lack of trust I adopted when I was given away to a man for marriage at a very young age, by my mother. The worse abandonment feeling there could have ever been for me because I so loved her and even idolized her as my hero because she worked so hard for the family and sacrificed so much for us as children, and then she became sick with cancer and it changed her life and every one of ours forever. For years I questioned everything, even the air I breathed; but I now know and understand that almost everyone at some point or time in their life wonders, "Who Am I?" It really doesn't matter what sort of childhood or life you come from. I know this question can bring in some dark feelings of loneliness and the feeling that no one understands you, not even yourself at times; I know I have been there. Today as a Survivor of so many trials this life, it has taught me to endure and overcome and that these feelings, and thoughts are what I now like to call, the *'chain of super natural callings'* and even though they don't feel like it, they are normal feelings; they can lead to many different self beliefs and bring forth the self doubts that are most of the time, 'not true,' to be answered and healed.

These questions and uncomfortable feelings are the place between you knowing your true self and not knowing your true self, and purpose or calling. The awkward emotion of (Where do I fit in? or Who am I?) but they are also the super natural calling to awaken your inner self to the light you hold within you, the light at the end of the tunnel so to speak; everyone searches for this knowledge for it is your soul calling out to you to become one with yourself, your purpose and destiny. There is a predestined plan written for each of us before we are even born and the longing we feel, is a key to the door of our planned, purposeful journey. It takes years sometimes to find out who we are at a core level and then there are others who are born just knowing.

I knew what my birth name was, where I was born, who my parents were, where I went to school, what I loved and what I disliked, and I even knew I loved God, but I did not know who I was at a core level or how deeply valued by God we all are. The evaluation of my-self I once held was just a very small percentage of 'who I truly am' at a core level, according to God.

I have come to understand that likes, dislikes, and all these other things are not who we are, as God's children. They are just part of what makes us who we are. I like blue jeans, but that is not who I am. It just means I like casual wear. I now years later realize I was in the middle of evolving into who and what I needed, and was meant to be. I knew as a teenager there was more to this life and that I had a calling but I did not believe I would ever find out what that was, and even if I did, the question remained if I was worthy enough to accept that calling; If my mother did not want me then how could anyone else and all of these uncomfortable feelings were buried deep within me for most of my life because I did not know who I was at a deep core level or even how to address it outside of prayer. But God does and God will bring you to it, to move you through it. Life and unfortunate circumstances come and at times we are not prepared for them because we are not solid at the core base within. Some of us are not taught as children how important it is to truly know ourselves on a deep personal level. How important it is to even be our own best friend. We are taught we have choices to like or dislike and that we need to strive to be as good if not better than someone else in order to succeed, but never to take the time to deeply and honestly know who we are inside our souls or to seek quite time and search for the meaning of our lives, and why we are here; So by the time we are out of school if we even get to go to school, I know I didn't, we are so caught up in the world that, we have lost ourselves and grow into adulthood feeling like something is missing; And there is, it is our connection with self and our connection to source.

As it is as natural to search and ask, "Who am I," it should be as natural to teach our youth to seek within for answers and become strong independent seekers of self acknowledgement and source. Lucky for me I knew about faith for in the end it taught me about knowing my true self. I share my stories every chance I get because I don't want another person to spend their life wondering, Who am I? Where do I fit in? Who needs me? What could I offer?

I want to tell you as you read this, the answer to these questions are as follows;

1. **You are God's child that is 'Who you are!'**
2. **You fit right where he has you growing from! There is a reason you are where you are and a purpose.**
3. **Life needs you and all you contribute by just being alive and being present, and being, You....**

You can offer the world all you know, survived and overcome along your journey, after all, you are proof, God exist each day you wake up and greet the day.

Know you are loved and know that no matter where you are or how bad it may be, the light to the way home is within, you already have the answer. Like the light house on the hillside, within its walls there is safety, warmth and hope. You hold within you the light of hope so bright that even faith the size of a mustard seed can grow.

Who would of thought that I would become a Professional Truck Driver and travel for years and then become an International & US Bestselling Co-Author 10+ times in my life, even without the schooling I missed, God recovered me and helped me to rediscover me and 'Who I Am!' He changed my 'Who Am I? to Who I Am!'

I was able to care for my mother until her passing from Alzheimer's and Dementia, and I wouldn't change a minute of my time with her no matter how painful it was on so many different levels, the healing continues today, but my love for her is stronger now than ever before. I miss her everyday but I take comfort in knowing we will be together again someday. Love and Light to you my friend and always know you are loved by God above, always and forever – Amen! Answer your Super Natural Calling and get ready for the chain of miracles to happen in your life. *He Is Alive!*

About the Author

Sharon Gulley is the owner operator of Beautiful Expectations of Faith and she lives in Jacksonville, Florida. Sharon is a multi-time anthology bestseller in combination of internationally and in the US. She has also written spiritual articles in the Wonderful online Tribute Magazine and at Linkedin.com, and at PATHEMagazine.com; an Amazing, Entrepreneurial Magazine. She studies in the field of Ministry, Spiritual Healer, and Metaphysical healing, and ancient medicine. She also works with Domestic Violence Survivors who suffer from PTSD and Shock Trauma coming out of Domestic Violence relationships. Sharon also works with finding your inner calling to purpose and to overcome any adversity life places before you. She is a retired Professional Truck Driver and a cancer survivor; she was once a full-time caretaker of her mother for 7 years, who pasted away in 2017 from complications of Alzheimer's and Dementia. She became an Author, Co-Author, Editor, Creative Writer, Motivational Speaker, Storyteller,

Photographer and Soul Healing - Light Worker, and the Minister and CEO, and Founder of Beautiful Expectations of Faith, while caring for her mother; She councils from her own life experiences of being a Domestic Violence Survivor twice over in her life and a Caretaker. Sharon writes and loves poetry. Her favorite Authors are James Agee, Robert Frost, Helen Keller, Emily Dickerson, Mark Twain and T. S. Elliot. Her stories can be read in one of the wonderful anthologies listed below.

Sharon's first publication was in a 2015 book called (The Butterfly Flutters By) – A Poetry book filled with life, love, childhood memories and stories told. This book can be found on Amazon.com in the Author section. Visit her Blog on her website at www.sharongulley/weebly.com where she writes and shares her love for poetry and photography. You can read some of her poetry on Poetrysoup.com, Author – Sharon Gulley.

Sharon's Domestic Violence Co-Authored writes include: From Fear to Freedom, Echo's in the Darkness and Women on a Mission – *Sisterhood of Stories*, I Am Beautiful, 3 P's of Success – *Purpose, Passion & Profit*, and The Beauty of Color - *Poetry & Prose Collection* and Breaking the Cycle- *No Longer Silent*, His Grace is Sufficient- *He turned my mess into a message*, Hearing God's Voice – *Above the Chaos,* with Women on a Mission Enterprises, LLC. All anthologies can be found on Amazon.com

Sharon Co-Authored in the Domestic Violence Anthology '*Resilient*' Compiled by Kellie Fitzgerald of IbbilanePress.com Publishing and Co-Owner of

PathMag.com alongside Co-Complier, Lisa James. The book was published in December 2016) Can be found on Amazon.com She is in the 3rd Angel Anthology (*Warrior Women with Angel Wings for the Soul*) with Sundi Sturgeon of Holistic light Rejuvenation Center as the Compiler and WOM Enterprises, LLC as Publisher. *Sharon's books and co-authored books can be found on Amazon.com*

You can find Sharon Gulley at:
www.facebook.com/pg/BeautifulExpectationOfFaith/
https://twitter.com/GreenilyGulley and
https://www.linkedin.com/in/sharon-gulley,

https://www.amazon.com/Sharon-Gulley/ or
www.weebly.com/sharongulley

DEARLY BELOVED
Tarsha R.Lynch

"Psalms 91:11 "For he will give his angels charge over me" to keep thee in all thine ways" (KJ)

Dearly beloved we are gathered here today to lay to rest our shame, fears, struggles, convictions, suicidal ideations, depression, and anything that has come against us. We now take control of our minds, bodies, souls, and lives. We are children of God, who dare to do what we set out to do and we aspire while inspiring others to reach their goals in life. We've challenged the oppressor, defied economic conditions, and paved ways for other people around the world who suffer in silence and shame. We dared to be different, we stand for justice, we believed we could and we did. We are the overcomers of abuse and a voice to and for the voiceless.

I entitled this chapter Dearly Beloved after reading one of my first rough drafts written over 8 years ago in which I had included my obituary. Those dark days are long behind me now. As I sit back and reflect on the last 27 years of my life, I am often perplexed by the different circumstances that I have faced. The good, bad, and the ugly. I would often hear stories about people being alcoholics, drug addicts, physical abuse, emotional abuse, and running through massive amounts of money or getting into bad relationships. I would say to myself damn- glad that isn't me or how did *"they"* let that happen?

Never knowing that there is a thin line, we all walk through between good, evil and temptation.

Never in a million years did I think that I'd be one of *"those"* people who suffered from domestic violence, alcoholism, prescription drug abuse, and financial instabilities. I did not know that those things would be a part of my journey and forever leave an artic chill on my soul. You see I thought that if you didn't get beat to a pulp and hospitalized that you weren't *"really"* abused. Or if you weren't locked up in a mental facility or received a SSI check that you weren't *"really"* suffering from mental illness or if you were prescribed a pain medication that you weren't *"really"* abusing the drugs. Oh and here is the best one—if you had a good paying job there was NO way in hell that you could be broke or become homeless. It wasn't until I became the person on the other side of those scenarios that I learned this thought process or ignorance was a lie. There's an old saying that ignorance is bliss and that it is. I found myself entangled into my very first domestic violence situation in my early 30's and again a few years later.

The first incident involved my ex-husband. We had gotten into a physical altercation due to our finances. Once the yelling, fighting, and screaming was over I found myself bruised. Bruised mentality, emotionally, physically, and financially. Since I wasn't beaten down to my knees or riddled with black eyes, or a multitude of bruises, I discounted the impact that the event would have on my life and my future. Remember, I thought, that you weren't allowed to claim that you were abused unless you almost died or got really close to it. If you did make that claim, you were a liar and a weak individual.

In fact, I did die that day and deep down inside I knew it. Pieces of me died and I never accepted it until years later. I can't help but wonder what kind of person I would have become or be *IF* that never happened. Shortly, thereafter I was diagnosed with PTSD. My stinking thinking allowed me to ignore the diagnosis, wing myself off the medicines and not attend therapy any longer. Years later, my now ex-husband and I had reconciled and were able to move beyond the ashes of the domestic violence and become dear friends.

Prior to this incident, I was told that therapy is or was for crazy people, people who didn't have anyone to talk to, people who suffered from low self-esteem, or rich people who had tons of loot to waste. Besides black people didn't go to therapy during those days. If they did it was not discussed or publicized. If it didn't kill you, hell it would make you stronger. Pull yourself up by your boot straps and get over it! And never, ever let the thought of suicide take growth. Besides that's not what strong people do. These are the lies that most of us tell ourselves. My mother always told me, you "know where you've been" but you don't know where you're *going*.

Years later after the domestic violence incident I found myself engulfed in a downward spiral of other addictions that included alcohol abuse and prescription pain killer abuse. It didn't seem like abuse at the time but a coping mechanism that I thought was absolutely normal. It never once crossed my mind that my over indulging in alcohol was abusive. Neither did I think that taking one to two extra Vicodin was abusive. I thought it was abusive when you could no longer mask it. It was abusive when you lost your job behind it, or had a run in with the law for drunk driving.

Other than that it was not abuse but life. I had allowed the abuse I experienced and the abuse I inflicted on myself to take up real estate in my mind which resulted in poor decisions and illogical behaviors. I valued others and relationships with others more than I valued myself. During my deepest, and darkest depressive states were the only times I valued myself or the lack there of value for myself. I often would compare my circumstances to other people's circumstances only to allow myself *NOT* to feel like I was abused, crazy, or deranged. I often blamed myself in almost every episode of abuse I experienced. Whether it was at the hands of a lover, friend, or family I always asked myself what I did to deserve it. Or what could I have done NOT to get abused.

In 2017-2018 I found myself in a verbally abusive relationship with a narcissist and I had reached my breaking point. During that time, I looked myself in the mirror and asked myself did I want to live or die? In the physical I wanted to die because I felt like I had already died in the spirit a long time ago. With tears streaming down my face, and snot dripping from my nose I answered *YES*. I knew once I answered *YES* to living that I had to do just that, *live*. I had finally decided that I wanted to live and that there was no price tag that could be put on my peace.

The moment you decide that your life matters is the moment when the beast in you will be awaken. It's in that very moment when you decide to love yourself, forgive yourself, pray for yourself, and encourage yourself that you find strength that you did not know was there. In the valley of realizing that you matter is when you'll be able to take pivotal steps to recovery. We often get lost in the sauce of the hustle and bustle of life that we forget who we are, and whose we are. In the moments of being abused we lose, self-worth and sometimes self-control.

Once I figured out that at my absolute best I still would not be enough for the *wrong person* and at my absolute worst I will be worth it for the right person, I was able to let go of past hurt. I had suffered from Empath Syndrome almost my whole life, not knowing what it was called other than "good hearted". I knew that good hearted people were often more susceptible to becoming a victim of abuse. However, I still thought that my upbringing, education, street knowledge, and military training wouldn't leave any room for fallacy in the abuse arena. But I was wrong in a sense, however those traits are what assisted me to win in the long run. Once I changed my mindset I began to win at the game of life, gain clarity, and create abundance. I now understand and accept that I have a place in this world and that I have complete authority over my life. I now understand that abusive people can no longer strip me of my authority and I will not allow events or circumstances to unknowingly take it over. I understand that I am and will always have to participate in my own rescue.

I believe that people who suffer from Empath Syndrome are often caregivers of love, time, money, and resources. They often run themselves raggedy and become subjected to the pestilence of the world. Empaths hear, and see the world, people, and places differently. If you identify with being an empathic person learn to say NO, protect your peace, protect your space and know that not everyone or everything deserves to be in your space. Preserve your energy for you and stop allowing people and circumstances to deplete you. I had to learn a new set of coping skills due to the trauma I endured at the hands of loved ones over the years. Getting back to me was a process and a journey I deal with daily. I had to understand and accept that I am worthy of peace, protection, living a life of abundance, and most importantly that I MATTER. To all of those who have suffered or are still suffering from some form of abuse I'd like to tell you that there is a light at the end of the tunnel, you are loved, and you are not alone and most importantly you MATTER.

About the Author

Tarsha Lynch is a mental health advocate, motivational coach, influencer, author, and TX Realtor. Her mandate is to inspire, support, and encourage those who struggle with mental illness such as depression, PTSD, anxiety, and stress by offering personalized mentoring or referrals to mental health professionals, coaches, and community programs connected to her colleagues in the AssistU2 Win tribe. Tarsha's a witty divorcee, a mother of 2 adult children (Amber and Benjamin) and a grandmother to Harley Drew. She is an active member of the *Potter's House Dallas* and holds multiple degrees and certifications. Find out more about Tarsha Lynch, the Get Your Lick Back Coach, @ iamtarshalynch.com, or on all social media platforms under Tarsha Lynch.

PURPLE RAIN
Tesha D. Colston

As I laid on my daughter's bed being pulled by my ankles by my husband into our bedroom, I wondered "How in the heck did we get to this point?" He was literally trying to have sex with me in her bed but my legs were strong and he needed more room so he pulled me by my feet through the hall and to the bedroom. I knew my daughter was pretending to be sleep. There is no way she could be sleep at this point. It was probably for the best for them that they all remained asleep. At this point it was like a demon had taken him over and there is no telling what could have happened. I recognize this demon and he had gotten stronger and stronger.

Hi my name is Tesha D. Colston and my first husband was verbally, physically and sexually abusive throughout our twenty-five years of marriage. I thought his behavior would change but it never did. I had no one to talk too. How could I discuss these things? I was ashamed and afraid and had no one coming to my rescue.

How it started

I was fourteen years old and for the first time my parents allowed my sister and I to go to the mall alone! We were so excited to be doing something on our own. Little did I know that this is where it would all began. On the train coming home from the mall I met this 21-year-old man and he walked with us home. I fell for this man. He was wonderful so I thought but how the heck would I really know, I was fourteen. We were extremely sheltered growing up. We grew up as Jehovah's Witness and we couldn't have 'worldly' friends or do 'worldly' things. To me life was just so unfair. We were monitored in every area of our lives, from friendships to movies to music to food. Holidays were way out the question.

The life my parents tried to shelter me from was the very life I ended up living. Now pregnant and sixteen, I was ready to move out! My mom would not allow us to move in together without being married so we married. We moved into a room together. I do not remember the first incident. I believe I still have mental blocks because I just cannot remember things even though I try really hard to remember. I do not remember the first time I was raped by my husband. I remember the jealousy that he had and it got worse and worse as time went on. I remember that we used to fight a lot. We fought because he was extremely jealous and he would accuse me of sleeping with anyone, from his uncle to his brother and that jealousy never ended. When he got into one of his bouts of jealousy, he would always want sex and there is where the tussles would begin and the fights would start. At the time I didn't know it was rape but I knew it wasn't right. I knew marriage wasn't supposed to be this way. I never saw my parents fight for sex and they were always in the room and we knew what they were doing. However, my married life was turning out not to be like theirs at all.

We had moved from the room into an apartment, and his mother and brother lived with us. His brother was rarely home but his mother was home most of the time. I think I believed that in some way his mother would be able to help but she never did. There was one time she did at least say something. It was Christmas time and it was the first time I could have a tree up. I don't remember why it happened but I can tell you that I didn't want to have sex and he did. We fought that day and it was so bad we ended up in the hallway. I remember that he stomped me in the face with his boot. I am not sure why she came out that time but she did and she said, "Damn, why don't you just leave the girl alone?" He never did and that was the first time the police were called. I don't remember who called them. That was the first of 3 orders of protection against him but I always went back.

Why didn't I leave?

Just like people wondered why those in domestic violence situations don't leave, I also wondered why I wouldn't just leave for good. Over the course of our marriage, I did leave a few times, I just didn't stay gone. I admit the times that I left was only after the police had been called and an order of protection was issued. He was very good at apologizing and begging me to come back. Also, as I look back, I never considered myself as a domestic violence victim. Besides it was all my fault, right? I mean if I would just have sex when he wanted most of this wouldn't have happen right? Then there is how to leave? What would I do? It wasn't that bad I thought. I made this bed and I need to lay in it.

Not to mention I had a child and a GED, the only thing I could do was go to my mother's but I just couldn't so I stayed. I kept getting pregnant and because I didn't want any more children, I would have abortions. I lost count on how many I had; I believe I had about 7 in the first 7 years of marriage. Now pregnant again I decided no more abortions, I will have my second child; By this time my mother had moved to Seattle, WA; and I decided I was moving and changing my life. I really didn't want him to come but he did.

As I settled into the idea that he was coming, I had built up hopes that moving would help him to change but he never did. He was so jealous he just accused me of sleeping with every man we knew. He wanted sex all the time and I wanted it none of the time. It was miserable. The physical abuse was never constant. The sexual abuse was never consistent. I had learned to give in and I stopped fighting, as much. One of my coping mechanisms throughout my marriage was drugs and alcohol which is what he introduced me to. We smoked a lot of marijuana, drank beer and alcohol, did cocaine and we would watch porn. See if I could just be in the mood I wouldn't get into trouble and so down that path of addiction I continued. I remember having a huge fight in our second apartment in Washington. I called the police and they came, and took him to jail. Washington police do not mess around when it comes to domestic violence issues. He spent the weekend in jail, which never happened in NY. I felt feel sorry for him and he came back home as it had happened every time before and every time after. Eventually, I started going to church and I found some peace in that. Maybe if I'm going to church it would stop. Maybe this foolishness would stop but it didn't; but at least I had someone else I could talk to, I now had God. Of course, I was sleeping with the people at the church, so he always said; but I had God to talk to now and a hope of something different somewhere after this mess was over.

I hoped God would protect me, maybe the more I attended church the more I would earn his protection but that was the wrong way to think and my situation did not change. I remember being so depressed and just not wanting to be here anymore by this time I had twins and now we had 4 children. I would fight off the thoughts of suicide. I had children to be here for. However, there is this one time that I remember getting up in the middle of the night getting a knife and coming back to the bed. I had enough of this life and I was going to end it. I was going to leave just not the way I should have left. So I lay down with the intent to slit my wrist and bleed out over the very bed I had, had so much pain in. I heard a voice that stopped me and it quoted a scripture saying, "Weeping may endure for a night, but joy cometh in the morning. If you hang on to the morning, you won't feel this way. Your problems won't have gone away but you won't feel this way." So, I put the knife down and went to sleep. This is the victory…. I got up!

How did it end?

I was in denial about the severity of my situation. I compared my situation to others. I mean I wasn't one of the women who had black and blue eyes and ended up in the hospital with fractures and swollen faces. No, this abuse, this pain no one could see. Society and church have very different views on this type of abuse. It was not ok to be not ok with sex in marriage. Your body is not your own. You should tell your husband yes, all the time. It's your fault. One day, my youngest son had brought home a pamphlet that talked about domestic violence. I read it. I remember that it listed out all the ways people are abused. Verbal and sexual abuse was on the list. It was then that I realized that I really was in domestic violence situation and I was a victim, that I was not alone, that this was not ok with everyone. Maybe I found validation in that little pamphlet. I had a conversation with the husband about it. I told him that what he was doing was actually rape and that he could go to jail for rape. He didn't believe me. I showed him the pamphlet. I think I had hopes that it would stop and we would have a normal relationship but it didn't. This time, during the act, I could tell him he was raping me, but that never worked. Fast forward to the day the washer broke and I needed to go to my cousin's apartment to wash clothes. I took one of my daughters with me. We had a lot of clothes and I was there for a long time. I don't know why I didn't go to the Laundromat, but we were there so long we all feel asleep and didn't get home until the next morning. I knew he would be upset but I didn't think he would be that mad after all I was washing our clothes and I had my daughter with me. He argued but the kids were home and I was like man you are tripping. The kids got ready for school and off they went. There's where the real arguing happened. I remember he had me pinned to the wall with his hands around my throat telling me he could kill me. I don't remember all the details. I just know the police were called. This time they didn't arrest him but he chose to leave. I had made the final decision; I was just done. I packed some things and off I went to my cousin's house. I stayed there and guess what he did? He filed for divorce and I never went back!

About the Author

Tesha D. Colston (aka) The Marketplace Evangelist has an unrelenting passion for evangelism. Her strong belief in the power of God, Jesus, and the Holy Spirit is Source, and substance of her success. Her experience as a Minister (Evangelist) Leader in Praise, Worship, and Women's Ministries and Sunday school has afforded her the ability to share messages filled with compassion and simplicity to her audience in a way that compels them to grow spiritually and naturally. Tesha D. Colston is married to Kenneth Colston and together has 6 children and 6 grandchildren.

NEVER GONNA GIVE UP
Veronica Pryor-Faciane

"Possible Trigger Warning"

Hello All! I am honored you are taking this precious time to read about my truth. I am sure someone or maybe every reader may resonate with this story in some form or fashion. In life, individuals sometimes face various forms of trauma and often wonder how to leave the hurt and anguish behind. Some may even believe their life does not matter. Have you ever felt as if you were a mistake or the world would be better off without your existence? Deeeep long slow breath! Sad to say, I felt this way most of my life.

You see, I suffered what some would call, insurmountable abuse. The person that abused me should have been one to protect me and show me how a lady should be treated as queen.

So, have you guessed who it was dear reader and yes, it was a close family member? Trauma brought continuous drama in all facets of my life mentally, physically, financially and spiritually. This unpleasant childhood trauma leading into adulthood started at the age of five for the next twenty-eight years. Oh, why Lordddd!!!! What the hell did I do to deserve this? I was told that if I did not want my mom sad that I should do as I was told. Okay, do you have a child or children? If not, you have an idea the statue and mental capacity of a five-year-old, I am sure. Yes, I am sure you may have a picture of who my perpetrator is. MY BIRTH-FATHER WAS MY ABUSER. How could he do this to his own flesh and blood? How could he hurt someone who looked up to him? How could he continue to hurt me even when I would show him I did not hate him? The true question is when was I going to wake up and realize I MATTERED?

Ladies, do you remember the imaginations you had at that age? You remember the hand games and playing jump-rope games you played? Well that did not matter to me. Hell, I did not matter to me. I just wanted to have peace at night. I just wanted my mom to protect me. But how can she protect me when he was abusing her just as much or even more. Ughhhhhh, this life 'Really' sucks! How would any child feel their life matters in this sort of condition? God must hate me to be allowing this type of travesty to be happening to an innocent child. Wait, I said it happened for over 28 years. It is sad how he conditioned me for this. He conditioned those who he should have been protecting and ministering to. Yes, I said he was a minister too. Go figure a man of God misusing his own family.

How could he do such a thing? Then once my little sister he strongly suggested I continued to listen to him if I did not want him to touch my little sister. Well he can't touch my baby, but around the time she made ten years-old, she told me he was touching her. I was hurt, in disbelief and scared. I told her it will be ok. Let's go tell mom. Everything was so much better after telling her. NOTTTTT!!! She was more fearful than we were it appeared.

I hated the "WHAT ABOUT ME" feeling. Speaking up for my-self was a challenge. I would just swallow any feelings I had. I was a good girl. I was on the honor roll and worked in various areas of community service. So, why was I feeling like I did not matter?

I used to see my birth-father crying on the side of the bathtub asking why his momma let this happen to him. Ok, so something tragic must have happened to him. I know he could barely read once he graduated from high school. It was so sad to hear him say his mother told him, "You are a stupid mother-fucker that won't be anything." I was the oldest child and I had to protect my siblings. No child would want to experience this within their family unit. This generational curse, challenge, problem or whatever the world calls it had to stop!!! I can't do this Noooo moreeeee.

I am grateful for having my own connection to "THE SOURCE." Even though I thought the connection was not there, overtime...ummm overtime things changed for me mentally.

Remember Romans 12:2 states, "And be not conformed to this world: but be ye transformed by the renewing of your mind, that ye may prove what is that good, and acceptable, and perfect, will of God. (KJV)

In my opinion, my birth-father professed having Christ-Like Qualities in public daily yet behind closed doors he was horrible. He never would admit he needed help mentally. I remembered, his oldest brother seeking out help, but not my birth-father. He persisted on saying nothing happened to him. I was directing choirs, and this gave me a since of peace. Yes, he started penetration around middle school, and I choose not to tell anyone outside of the house for fear. He taught us what went on in his house stayed in his house. He threatened impregnate me if I did not comply. If I did tell, what would happen to my siblings? What if we are put into a foster home and things become worse? What if we are separated and I don't see them ever again? What ifs were coming from everywhere? My sister was married first. Then my next two brothers moved out.

Ok, I may be able to get out finally. I am tired of him taking my money and using sexually. I think I am starting to see that I Matter. He had my mom so scared of him. He was angry most of the time. There were times when my mom appeared to be mad at me for the things going on within our home. I was so confused and hurt. I guess I don't matter.

"I wish I could have lived a balanced and happy childhood. However, my life was filled with plenty of dysfunction. I wish I could have attended parties and other functions like my peers, but due to the daily drama, he did not allow us much freedom or distance from him. I was forced to live with a caged mind, heart, and soul. I would see my classmates' prom pictures and wish I could have had that opportunity. I cried for never having a chance to be a child, for never experiencing prom, if only for one night." (Veronica Pryor-Faciane, March 2019)

God knows how to get your attention and after marring my king on June 12, 2004 and having 3 sons I was tired of living in darkness.

I had to go to get help for my PTSD, ADHD, Depression, Anxiety and Stress I was experiencing daily. No, I still did not matter to me yet. I decided to go to outpatient therapy and find out who Veronica was as an individual. My children and my husband were the main reasons I sought out help. My actions affected them developmentally. I had to determine what I desired to accomplish as part of my life's journey after trauma? It began with a single step towards my next. Oh, I did not have my husband's support at first. I was sick and tired of just existing. How about you? What type of trauma have you experienced, and you are deciding to change the negative direction your family has been going towards? What if you don't have the support of those closest to you? Would you stop? Well, would you? Most people would and there are many days I have this feeling within my belly. Just give it up. Life would be easier Veronica.

It took just one spark to start a fire. Now, I am singing won't HE do it…..this girl is on fire….Yessss! Even when I sometimes get mentally drained! I KEEP PUSHING TOWARDS MY NEXT!

You can be on fire as well with just starting to change your mindset one negative thought at a time. With therapy and a change in my mindset I used the knowledge to elevate and eradicate the garbage that was downloaded within me by my birth-father. Yes, I pressed charges trying to save my mom. He went to jail; however, she was still imprisoned mentally and stopped eating for 2 months. I truly have learned that my self-love and self-esteem. My mom transitioned on March 23, 2015 to her heavenly home. Now, I am choosing to be a transformational coach, speaker and author for those that feel as if there is no hope after domestic violence or incestuous abuse. I am a living example of how Your Best Is Yet to Come when you learn how to live on top of your story and no longer drown within your story. Queens and Kings, always remember YOU MATTER.

Reference

Pryor-Faciane, Veronica, (2019). God's Diamond In the Rough.

About the Author

Veronica Pryor-Faciane is the CEO/Founder of New ID Life Coaching LLC. This wife and mother of four beautiful children authored God's Diamond in The Rough (released March 2019) and co-authored the newly released anthology For a Mother's Heart (released May 2019). Due to her passion for inspiring others, she will be included within 2 more anthologies due to release in the 3rd and 4th quarter of this year. Veronica continually utilizes her voice without hesitation to impart the needed information to ignite elevation and transformation within the hearts of those who have been made to feel as if they are in a period of mental, physical and possible financial stagnation due to domestic violence.

She continues to speak on platforms where she vocalized her truth:

- Honored to receive the Butterfly Society Award from The Butterfly Society October 2019, one of the local Domestic Violence Agencies in the Baton Rouge area.

- The very 1st black woman's mental health 4 city tour called Crazy Like a Fox, where she spoke in Atlanta, Ga. & Baltimore, MD in 2019.
- The ICAN Woman's Gala 2019.
- Assist U2 WIN Winsday Experience in Arlington, Texas 2019.
- X-Pose Domestic Violence Authors Forum 2019.
- Casual Conversations Live Broadcast -Now Church 2019.
- Featured in Swagher Magazine's Author's Spotlight 2019.
- Broken Hope Foundation Domestic Violence Forum 2018.

Those who choose to take the journey of reading about her truth, enrolling in online self-help courses or attending workshops have the possibility of gaining the tools and techniques to begin to restructure those negative thoughts, memories and emotions gained from the abuse suffered.
You can begin to heal from depression, anxiety, stress and control suicidal thoughts that plaque them on a daily, weekly and sometimes minute by minute basis.

It is her daily mission, to serve as a guide for others desiring to thrive and not just survive along life's journey.

She assists them in developing a successful roadmap towards their NEW ID and not the identification that was given to them by their parents, environment or various societal factors. This passion was invoked after developing a ***warrior and not worrier mindset***, overcoming 28 years of incest, financial, physical, spiritual and domestic violence suffered at the hands of her ministerial birth-father.

Veronica graduated from Grand Canyon University fall 2018 with her master's degree in Psychology with a Concentration in Life Coaching. Veronica has always strived for excellence despite life's adversities by accomplishing the following:

- Graduating from Xavier University of New Orleans with honors in 1994, President of Xavier University's National Association of Black Accountants, member of Alpha Kappa Mu Honor Society, a member of Who's Who Among Students, selected to participate in a Graduate Internship during my Junior year of collage at Notre Dame University, and other academic distinctions.

Veronica has worked with in various facets in God's Kingdom (i.e. teaching during Vacation Bible School several years, directing choirs and planning events such as a Back to School Rally among a few.)

Her passion for helping those that have experienced various traumas throughout life has assisted in her continuous healing journey. She is no stranger to the challenges of dealing with depression, anxiety and has attempted suicide.

She is a living example of how restructuring negative thoughts via mindfulness can pave the way to living your best life.

- Control your thoughts or they will control every aspect of your life (beliefs, actions and habits).

- Remember, your BECOMING depends on YOU taking Daily Positive Action.

- Your Peace matters begin & end each day with the attitude of gratitude No Matter What! Obstacles comes your way.

A *Positive Mindset* & monitoring your internal *G.P.S. (Guarding your Psychological Steps Daily)* is key towards evolving into the precious gem "YOU DESIRE TO BE."
~ Veronica Pryor-Faciane, MS

Contact Information

Email addresses: NewIDLifeCoaching888@gmail.com
Social Media Information:
Website: https://www.newidlifecoaching.com/
Facebook: https://www.facebook.com/veronica.faciane
Instagram: https://www.instagram.com/newid888/

Links to purchase E-books:
Books2Read.com/GodsDiamondintherough

Amazon Kindle version: https://amzn.to/2WZFPUs
Purchase on Amazon paperback version:
Bit.ly/Godsdiamond
For those desiring a signed copy, they can reach out to
Veronica via email

MY JOURNEY
Wanda Edwards

In the beginning….

I saw his temper and how mean he could be, but it was never directed towards me. I would always feel protected when I was with him. In the beginning it was fun, it was loving, and I was happy. In the beginning it was good.

I have learned in hindsight that I was already in emotional pain, when I met him. I just wanted desperately to be loved. My father died when I was nine and my earliest memories of him is during the time that he was sick. I am told, I would have learned a lot from him. I was told he loved his family and was a proud husband and father. I believe if he had lived, I would have made different choices in men.

I had 2 older brothers at the time, the oldest is also deceased and an older sister. I was what they called at the time a change of life baby, so my siblings and cousins, were all much older than me some by 15 years. So, I was practically an only child. After my father died, my younger brother took it hard and he was not around for many years. I grew up without positive male role models. Sexually molested at the hands of 2 of my uncles and that did not help my perception of men and women relationships. As a result, I was very promiscuous during my teen years, sex meant love to me. I wanted to be loved.

When I was sixteen, I had a saline abortion that means I was over 4 months, labor was induced, and the baby was aborted into a bed pan. It was the second traumatic experience I would experience, the first being the death of my father. I left a huge piece of my body, mind and soul in that hospital bed. I was never the same. No one knew or cared to know that much about depression at that time. You did what you had to do, got over it and kept it moving.

So, when I got married, I believed that I was leaving those hurts behind me, not knowing a bigger one was coming. The first time he hit me, I remember simply thinking 'as he was slapping me openhanded over and over across my face and just before the punch' "What is happening? Am I getting hit? Is this real? It can't be."

We were both getting ready for work. He asked me to iron his shirt. I told him I didn't have time, I was running late. I had my back to him, so I didn't see the anger building; I didn't notice the change in his voice with each request. Then I was on the floor, blood on my hands, feeling an emotion that to this day I still can't explain. A combination of fear, confusion, pain and anger. I sat there, for what seemed forever, mainly because I had no idea what to do.

As quickly as it started, it ended. I went in the bathroom and looked in the mirror. What the hell was I looking at? Is this my face? Why is my eye half shut? I need it to open more so I can see better, but it wouldn't, it was injured. It would be a long time before I really 'saw' myself again. I subconsciously avoided mirrors after that day; other than a quick glance to make sure my hair was combed, and makeup looked ok, 'Another traumatic experience that changed my life forever.' Over the next 6 or 7 years we had two daughters and a few happy moments. He never hit me in my face again. He would punch me in my stomach or back, choke me until I passed out, pull my hair, push me, cut my hair with an army knife, and threaten to kill me. I truly had no idea what happened to my life, my family did what they could, my friends were pretty much non-existent. I went to work, took care of my daughters and hoped I wouldn't be abused. I had become a shell, robotic, kind of just going through the motions. One night, he made me take all my clothes off, he poured alcohol (I think it was rum, or scotch) on me, sat on top of me and lit matches. My daughters were in the next room sleeping. I remember saying goodbye to them in my heart and mind. There was an overwhelming feeling of surrender, sadness, fear and defeat. I believed I was going to die that night. It was crushing me. I fainted.

I never looked at that night as surviving anything that would have been too much to have to bear. I simply referred to it as the night he "poured alcohol on me and lit matches". It was years later before I could call it what it was "the night I almost died." I began to drink alcohol, take pills and smoke marijuana to cope with the reality of my situation. I lived in constant fear of the next attack and my day to day living was trying to make sure I didn't do anything to trigger any abuse. I tried numerous times to leave, but he would always find me, and I would always go back. It would be two years later that I would finally get out. I did not know about "safety planning" at the time however in hindsight it's exactly what I did. My brother was getting married and I knew this was my opportunity because he would not be going.

The three weeks before the wedding my mother and aunt would come, while he was at work and remove clothes and toys. I decided this was it for me and I was leaving for good. The days leading up to the wedding I was a nervous wreck, fearing he would realize things were missing, but he never said a word. The morning of the wedding my cousin arrived to pick me up, as we were leaving, he took my daughters "as if he was saying goodbye," but instead moved them away from me. He told them to go in the bedroom and informed me that I could leave but they were staying.

He had also cut the dress I was going to wear so I had nothing to wear to the wedding at this point. I understood this was his way of making sure I returned from the wedding. I knew he would not hurt the children, but I also knew I could not leave them because I had no intention of returning. I pleaded with him to let me take them; I tried to reason with him that my family would certainly be looking to see them with me. He would not give in and as it escalated, I stopped asking and told my cousin we should just leave. My daughters were crying and I tried to comfort them and let them know mommy would be back soon. I left with my cousin and went straight to the police station. When I got to the police station, I explained that my husband would not let me take my children out of the house and I was afraid for them and me. This was another turning point for me. After a few minutes, a very big, very scary police officer approached me and said "Ok, Mrs. Edwards lets go get your daughters." Now, this officer had everything he needed, size and weapons; however, the level of fear that I had for my husband made me feel that he needed back-up. In my mind we needed a whole SWAT team to take this man down.

This was the moment I began to realize that my abuse was not just physical; it was mental and emotional as well. The response of the officer was one that I never forgot, because he validated my fear and without making me feel judged or crazy, he asked me "How many more officers do you think we need, Mrs. Edwards?" I replied I didn't know. He went in the back and got another officer, asked me to trust them and then took me to get my daughters. We arrived back at the apartment; my husband came to the door as if nothing was wrong.

I was able to get my daughters and to my brother's wedding. We had to stop at a rest stop on the way to finish getting dressed, but we made it and had a great time. While my brother was on his honeymoon, my daughters and I stayed at his house along with my mother to plan my next steps. At this point, everyone knew how dangerous my husband could be and that he surely would kill me if he ever found me again. I was so scared and confused. I could not hold a single coherent thought; this was really my life right now? I had two beautiful daughters and I was determined to be around to raise them. I didn't know anything about domestic violence at the time it was referred to as battered women syndrome. I honestly don't remember how I got the phone number to the shelter; I just remember calling and speaking to Vanessa. Walking into that shelter with my daughters three days later was surreal. I was so lost and confused and truly just a shell of the woman I once was.

I didn't know there were other women that went through what I did. I never knew the extent of my isolation; it was just the life I lived. I stayed in the shelter for 3 months and while I learned a lot about abuse, I didn't learn anything at all about coping and a life after abuse. On March 3, 2001, I started my recovery process from drugs and alcohol; another period of darkness and despair. The only difference was that this abuse was self-inflicted, and I had learned to justify my self-destructive behavior. I simply didn't want to remember, feel or deal. Over the last 16+ years I have grown, learned, evolved, kicked and screamed, cried, had major bouts of depression. I literally clawed my way back to a life worth living. I would learn that he had demons as well as an addiction to heroin. There was a brief period of him trying to contact me again, but his addiction took him deeper and deeper into the streets and further away from me. There are periods of time that I don't remember; I had to come to terms with the fact that I would never be the same. I had to let go of the shame and guilt about what happened to me, accept that all things happen for a reason and that my journey had to go just as it did.

About the Author

She is referred to as 'The Repairer of the Breech,' by her former Pastor. Wanda began the first Volunteer Ministry for Women in crisis transition at her church in 2005. In was shortly after, that she became a licensed minister. She continues to facilitate powerful and relevant seminars and workshops for women and young girls.

In 2017, she was the recipient of the Phoenix Award for her "Strength, Courage and Resiliency," presented by Harambe Services Inc. In 2018 Wanda was honored by S.O.F.I.A for her "Outstanding Work and Dedication," received a Community Advocate of the Year Award by the Power of Women Summit and a Certificate of Recognition Award for her play "Not Just October" by Gamma Phi Delta Sorority Inc.

Wanda is the producer of a short film "Colors of Survival" which premiered in October 2016, the film reflects on the very harsh realities of domestic violence but is focused on the HOPE of surviving. "Not Just October," the stage play; which premiered to two sold out audiences in 2018; is the sequel that focuses on the need for continued discussion around the harsh and sometimes fatal effects of Domestic Violence. She volunteers with S.O.F.I.A, is a member of Arizona and New Jersey National Coalitions against Domestic Violence.

Wandaedwards48@yahoo.com,
IG @uniquelywanda
FB Wanda Edwards

MY STORY
Barbara Jewel Sides-Johnson

I met my abuser in high school, he was two years older than me. He was a friend of my older brother. He seemed loving and likeable. Young love sometimes does not know what is coming in the future. It has been forty-two years but I can still remember like it was yesterday. And those scars are still on my heart. We heal from it but we do not forget it.

We married when I was only seventeen years old. My ex-husband went into the US Navy one year after we married. We moved away from our families when he entered the military. That is when the physical abuse began. Prior to that it was only emotional abuse.

Emotional abuse we are so quickly to dismiss, but it is abuse and it leaves scars. But we do not count it as abuse. A lot of the time is the first step in the progression into physical abuse.

It Begins.

We lived in Brunswick, Maine on the first assignment away from our families. His first rage of violence was when he totally demolished the windshield of our truck by kicking it from the inside. I had not seen him act this way. It should have been a sign, a red flag, a premonition of things to come. But I was young and naïve.

He was convinced that his friend (another military serviceman) and I had romantic intentions for each other which was totally not the case. This was completely in his mind. It was not true! He had convinced himself, that it was a fact and he reacted in rage.

Another incident, while we were married. When we were stationed in Jacksonville, Florida the physical violence and emotional violence escalated as did his excessive drinking. I told him I wanted to start taking college classes there. His response was; "I'm not wasting my money to send you to college. You are too stupid to learn anything." More on that... I would prove him very wrong.

During the two years there the violence was primarily shoving, yelling and cussing at me. The military would have put him in the military jail. His commander was very involved in his squadron's lives. His wife invited the wives over for social get togethers. I confided with his commander about the drinking and violence. I do believe this kept it from being any worse. He was put in a drug and alcohol treatment program but he didn't have any improvement.

I left him once and went to my parents' home in Arkansas for about a month when our son was six weeks old. He begged and made promises until I returned back. Millions ask why we don't leave and why we go back. But until you have been in these shoes, you will never understand. I loved him and we had a child. I wanted my marriage and my family to work. And I was young. He was then released from the Navy with a dishonorable discharge due to his excessive drinking, I should have seen this coming.

We then moved to Tulsa, Oklahoma. My sister and her husband lived in the area but that didn't make any difference to him. The violence escalated to punching and hitting. His drinking was escalating too. One episode was particularly bad. His mother was in town visiting. I was at my sister's home and he came there because he wanted to take our son to see his mother. I normally wouldn't care however he was very drunk. He wouldn't let me drive. So, I told him he wasn't taking the baby. He tried to take the baby out of my arms. My sister took the baby and I was physically stopping my husband from getting to the baby. It ended with him bloodying my face & he left without our son. He ended up wrecking and rolling over the car. I'm grateful our son wasn't in the car with him.

I finally had enough and told him to leave. I didn't want my son to be raised in that environment. That is when the violence escalated to him trying to kill me with a butcher knife. When I was going out the door he yelled; "You better get back in here or I'll kill the baby." In that instant I had to decide what to do. I felt that if I went back in there was a very good chance our son and I would both be killed.

He had never been violent toward our son despite being very neglectful to not watch him properly. I ran to the neighbor's house and called the police. When the police arrived, they asked me "What did you do to make your husband want to cut your throat with a butcher knife". They put him in the squad car which allowed me to go in and get my son and get some clothes. There was a lady who was a co-worker and lived in my neighborhood. I went to her home for the night. I filed for a divorce after that. My younger brother came to live with me for a few months on my parents' insistence. When he moved back home my ex-husband showed up again threatening me.

I was DONE! I told him to leave and if he showed up at my door one more time, I had a rifle and would blow his head off. I would take my chances in court. I had shot a gun only once in my life! He never threatened me again after that.

My Words to other Women

Don't rush into relationships. Don't put yourself in situations where you are isolated from family. Always have access to your own money. If you do find yourself in an abusive relationship seek out help early. Don't believe what he says to destroy your self-esteem. However, for the sake of all the people who truly are in an abusive relationship please don't say you are in abusive relationship when you and your spouse just argue and don't agree. Abuse is when one spouse use power and control over the other spouse.

About the Author

I am now married for 33 years to a wonderful man. John adores me & I like being adored so we make a pretty good couple. He has supported me through going to college & getting my degree as a Legal Assistant.

I GRADUATED WITH A 3.9 GPA while working full time & being a mom & wife. John adopted Brian when he was 6 years old & we had our other son Bradley when Brian was 9 years old. We now have five grandchildren.

I am the owner of Legal Organization LLC & an independent consultant for Rodan and Fields skincare brand.

Printed in Great Britain
by Amazon